Holy Play Power Boosters
Declarations to Energize Your Commitment and Desire

Kirk Byron Jones

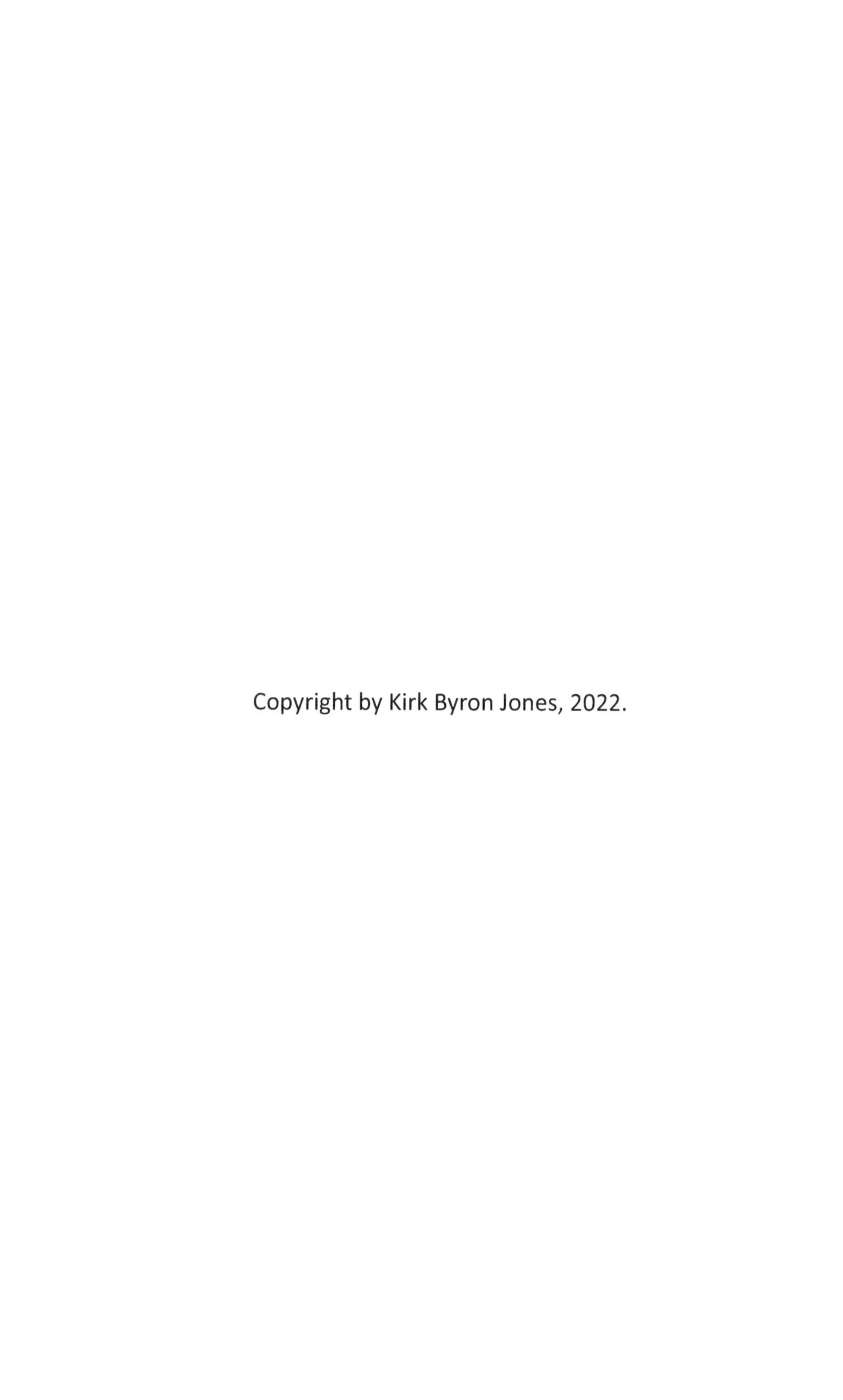

Contents

*"Words are powerful
when chosen well
and hurled with
precision."*

~~Nnedi Okorafor

*When you are
truly convinced
that words are
powerful, you
use them with
greater care
and expectancy.*

~~Kirk Byron Jones

Introduction

Some of the most memorable words I have ever received regarding one of my presentations are as follows:

As I was listening to you, I felt –I'm talking physically—arms go around my shoulders. It was a feeling of protection, one of "Fear not! For I am with you." It was a deep hug, like a shield.

It lasted awhile—I'm not sure how long. And then the feeling changed to one of friendship, as you put your arm around someone as a gesture of love. And again the feeling of "Fear not! For I am with you."

Words have such power, but I have never felt the physical power of words.

Have you ever felt the physical power of words, a noticeable bodily reaction due to what you heard or said?

As a boy preacher, I grew up understanding how moving words could be during a worship experience. Congregants at Mt. Herman Baptist Church in New Orleans, Louisiana didn't just hear the preaching, they responded to it in real time with shouts of affirmation and gestures of encouragement.

As time passed, through reading and living, I began to understand that words spoken privately to oneself could regulate attitudes and feelings. Words could change the way I experienced life.

I believe this now more than ever. And that is why this book is in the world. I know the words you will read can be transformative because they have changed and continue to change me.

The better you become at observing your thoughts and feelings, the greater your ability to mine and mold them to create your best life. Holy play within determines holy play without. There is nothing more influential to our thoughts and feelings than what we say to ourselves, our words.

Why not speak life over and over and over again?

Kirk Byron Jones
August, 2022

1.

I Live
with
Lavish Openness
and
Radical Receptivity!

2.

I Play
With
Patient Enthusiasm
and Relaxed Confidence!

3.

A consequence of
continually and
deliberately evolving
is being on alert
for capacities
and capabilities
newly available to you.

4.

I look
to
proven
inspirations
to urge
me on.

5.

You
were
born
to
play
and
soar.

6.

What's
in me
is greater
than
what's
against me.

7.

The Sacred Seven

1. I am God's Child.
2. I Play and Soar in the Spirit.
3. I Cocreate My Life with My Thoughts, Words, and Actions.
4. I Enjoy, Explore, and Expand.
5. I Join Others in Building the Beloved Community.
6. I Practice Enlightened Persistence.
7. It is Well with My Soul.

8.

Soul Talk Steps

Be Still.
Lay Burdens Down.
Listen Deeply.
Don't Run Away.
Be Honest.
Be Gentle.
Welcome New Truth.

9.

Just
because
you're in
a storm
doesn't
mean
the storm
has to be
in you.

10.

The deepest
reassurance
of all
is the
smile
of your
soul.

11.

Know
what fills
you
and what
drains
you.

Take
lavish
portions
of what
fills you.

12.

I live
with
ever-increasing
clarity,
intention,
confidence,
and joy.

13.

All things are possible to those who believe.
~~Mark 9:23

14.

I
am
at home
in the
grace
of my
being.

15.

The
saving
is in
the
savoring.

16.

Peaceful Pace Affirmation

I clarify
my priorities
and regulate
my pace
from a
space of
inner peace.

17.

You will be like a well-watered garden, like a spring whose waters never fail.

~~Isaiah 58:11

18.

7 Favorite Inspirations

Soul
Stillness
Prayer
Play
Journaling
Jazz
Just Being

19.

Cultivate
an intentional,
sustained
awareness
of your
being and
becoming.

20.

I
practice
fierce
intention
with a
light touch.

21.

Graduation is not just a celebratory public event. Notice personal moments of sure transition when you have unusually satisfying feelings of culmination and anticipation at the same time.

22.

Learn from Lazarus

After he was resurrected, Lazarus had to choose to get into the new life that had gotten into him.

Refuse to redress yourself in the grave clothes of deathly thoughts, beliefs, and behaviors.

Resist returning to that which drained you dry.

Trust the fresh thoughts, beliefs, and actions that give you new life.

23.

Take
your
time.

Notice.

Savor.

24.

Deepening
clarity is
available
the more you
make yourself
available
for listening within.

25.

I
value
my
treasure.

26.

Grace
has
me
covered.

27.

I
take
charge
of
my
energy.

28.

Sometimes the creative breakthrough is not doing something new, but doing something you have been doing with greater awareness and concentration.

29.

It
is
my
holy
calling
to
thrive.

30.

Simply Abiding

Free of
any expectation,
simply abiding
in stillness
heals us, and
brings us
home.

31.

I
resist
being
suspicious
of
overflow.

32.

The
deeper
wealth
is in
the cherishing.

It's not
what you hold
but what you
hold dear
that matters most.

33.

Refuse
to
be
afraid
of
your
flourishing.

34.

Stillness
gives us
the time
and space
to form
beautiful
questions.

35.

I am
not
afraid
of living
life
in full
bloom.

36.

Creativity
is the
outrageous
overflow
of a
joyous
soul.

37.

I
let
play
light
up
my
life.

38.

Don't
be
afraid
to
fly.

39.

Whatever
path
you
choose,
God
is
with
you.

40.

**5 Ways to Celebrate
Meaningful Completion**

1. Stop.
2. Notice.
3. Savor.
4. Be Thankful.
5. Feel Joy.

41.

Let
yourself
love
madly.

42.

Inspiration
is
the
universe.

43.

You
can
burn
bright
without
burning
out.

44.

No
matter
how
deep
the
hurt,
God's
Love
is
deeper.

45.

Do not
be afraid of
holy devotion.

Sacred passion
is powerful.

46.

Plan the Play;
Play the Plan!

47.

"Our ability to grow is directly proportional to an ability to entertain the uncomfortable."
~~Twyla Tharp, Choreographer

48.

The
hidden
movement
of stillness
is your soul
dancing
with God.

49.

What if
God is
playing
hide and
seek and
has hidden
in you?

50.

I choose
to be
at peace
with my
offering,
and let it
be well
with my soul.

51.

I expect
meaningful
insight
and
wisdom
from
my soul.

52.

Receive Grace

God's grace gives us the strength to face the unfaceable: a truth you don't want to believe; a hurt that won't go away; a dream that won't come true; a hope that feels broken; a life that seems lost. Such grace is not earned or won; just be open.

God need not be named to be known or invited to be present.

53.

To get
lost
in the
peace
of God
is to feel
fully found.

54.

Getting a Prayer Through

How do you talk to God
when you don't feel like it?

When life gets too heavy.

When people let you down.

When you think you've failed.

When God seems gone.

How do you get a prayer through
when you are through with prayer?

Be still.

Own your feelings.

Let your hurt speak.

Listen.

Prayer is not just what's said;
Prayer is what's heard.

55.

To forgive
is to stop
holding space
for letting
bitterness
linger longer
than it should.

56.

Rid yourself
of burdens
that were
never yours
to carry
in the
first place.

57.

"Look about you. Take hold of the things that are here. Let them talk to you. You learn to talk to them."
— *George Washington Carver, an African American agricultural scientist and inventor who invented 300 uses for peanuts.*

58.

Greatest Passion

May no
other passion
come before
your passion
for life
itself.

59.

There
are
always
other
levels
to get
to.

60.

Learning
alone
doesn't
grow us;
we grow
by living
what we learn.

61.

Knowing
how
matters.

Take
your
time
learning
the
process.

62.

Allow
yourself
long moments
to feel
the Spirit
urging
you on.

63.

If you are
ever arrested
for inciting joy,
make sure
there is
enough evidence
to convict you.

64.

Notice
and
honor
that which
calls forth
your deepest
strengths.

65.

I
Imagine,
Design, and
Create
My
Life
On
Sanctified
Purpose!

66.

It's not
just about
resisting rushing;
it's about
embracing noticing:
appreciating
the showing
in the slowing.

67.

Blessing Power

May mounting
awareness of
your blessings
be energizing.

Embrace
blessings
to bless.

68.

Even
if it's
small,
thank God for
visible progress
and
verified growth.

69.

Sometimes
the highest
calling
of all
is to
bask
in completion.

70.

Inner Holy Play

The better
you become
at observing
your thoughts
and feelings,
the greater
your ability
to mine and
mold them
to create
your best life.
Holy play
within
determines
holy play
without.

71.

WONDER.
QUESTION.
CONNECT.
CREATE.
REPEAT.

72.

Remember Resurrection

Because
love
raised,
you
can
live
lifted.

73.

I remain
alert for
waves
of insight
that may
arrive at
any moment.

74.

Relax.
God
never
intended
for you
to live
clenched.

75.

Knowledge
and skill
would often
fall flat
were it
not for
adaptability.

76.

Tenacious Insistence

Imagination
and intention
may be
left stranded
without the
arrival of
tenacious insistence.

77.

Be
clear
and
convinced
about
what
deserves
your
tenacious
insistence.

78.

I am
Blessed,
Beloved,
and
Worthy.

79.

Knowing
yourself
to be
blessed,
beloved,
and worthy
empowers you
to see others
in the
same light.

80.

STAY

PLAYFUL!

81.

Keep
asking,
"What if?"
and taking
your answers
seriously
in a delightful
sort of way.

82.

Look to
see it
as it is.

Look again
to see it
as it can be.

83.

I give
myself
permission
to
take
things
apart.

84.

Holy
Play.

Holier,
Playfully.

Wholly
Playful.

85.

I
value
and
live
the
wisdom
of
my
soul.

86.

The Soulful Seven

1. Take Your Time, Notice, and Savor.
2. Receive, Believe, and Live Soul Wisdom.
3. Be Fully Present.
4. Envision and Engage Labor as Holy Play.
5. Love Leisure.
6. Live Lavishly Open and Radically Receptive.
7. Feel Blessed.

87.

Morning Invitation

Come
baptize
yourself
afresh
in the
grace
of God.

88.

Notice
and
attend
to the
new
callings
within.

89.

When you feel like your efforts are unseen, be encouraged.

Sometimes lack of appreciation has more to do with limited capacity than deliberate choice.

Persons don't prize what they can't recognize.

90.

What if
the very
thought
of you
delights
God
so very much?

91.

Notice
what
makes
your
soul
smile.

92.

Your soul
will often
nudge you
when it's time
to raise
your level
of expectation.

93.

I feel
myself
changing
and intentionally
choose
to lean into
my transformation.

94.

Sufficient Solace

In the
wilderness
moments of
not knowing
what, when
where, or how,
God knows.

~~~~~~~~

Sometimes
the only thing
keeping you
and keeping
you going
is trusting
that God knows.
~~~~~~~~

95.

Enjoy
wandering
about
strange
new openings
and possibilities.

96.

Embrace
the
inspiration
in
the
process.

97.

May you
find most
of your days
to be
new,
different,
and irresistible.

98.

Notice
moments
when
you
feel
more
alive
than
usual.

99.

To see life as holy play is not to deny hurt, pain, and suffering, but to tenaciously embrace anticipation, engagement, and fulfillment through it all.

100.

Silly, Succulent Life

A new employee took the receipt and began processing my clothing pick-up at the cleaners. The store manager, always so pleasant, stepped out from the rear, greeted me, and started observing her trainee. At one point, the trainee looked at her manager for guidance proceeding with the transaction.

That's when it happened.

The manager tightened her mouth, raised her head, and looked away. The trainee was on her own.

After a brief pause, I started laughing. We all did.

The manager played the fool so her trainee could figure it out. And to our gleeful satisfaction, she did.

It was a side, unscheduled, unimportant moment of silly, succulent life.

Who are we without such lighthearted, strangely enchanting intrusions?

Who might we be, and become, noticing and savoring them more?

101.

Never
hesitate
to unleash
your full powers
regarding that
to which
you feel
divinely called.

102.

"What
would
I do
without
the absurd
and
the fleeting?"

~~Frida Kahlo

103.

Remember
moments
of being
saved, and
live them
again when
needing to
come back
to life.

104.

Jazz
is not
just for
listening;
Jazz
is for
living.

105.

Try not to
just play;
enjoy
playing.

106.

Trust
your
journey.
You were
living in grace
before you
realized it.

107.

The rhythms
of your life
are not
only what
you hear,
but what
you create.

108.

"…the future has an appointment with the dawn."
~~Tanella Boni

109.

Hold On

Sorrow's
word
though
deep
and full
is never
last.

110.

Especially the Heavy Heart

You must
give sadness
its due.
God is
everywhere
especially
the heavy heart.

111.

Sufficient Provocation

Waking up slowly
is sufficient provocation
to start you off
feeling blessed.
And sometimes
just waking up
is enough.

112.

There is
no rule
against
splashing
in the waters
of God's
grace.

113.

Fill
your
day
with
as many
inspirations
as possible.

114.

Holy Play Prayer

Dear God,

Grant me easy peace
in uneasy vulnerability,

as I resist being too comfortable
with overly precise understandings of you,

knowing that it is your playful will
to surprise me over and over again.

Amen.

115.

God
works wonders
in
awhile moments.

Be grateful
for those
who bless you
enormously
for a while.

116.

Don't
just create
the life
you want;
create
the life
you need.

117.

Curiosity,
playfulness,
and daring
will take you
a long way.

118.

Holy Acceptance Affirmation

Divinely
and
fully
affirmed,
I live freely
from acceptance
and not for it.

119.

There are
times
when you
can and
should
make your
load lighter.

120.

Don't
shrink.
Walk
upright
in your
blessings.

121.

What
is
my
soul
calling
me
to
set
aside?

122.

How
do
I
make
my
living
load
lighter?

123.

Sustained
devotion
to a
soul desire
is its own
fulfillment.

124.

The more
in touch
you are with
your soul,
the clearer
and surer
you are
in life.

125.

Suspicious Prayer

Praying
that appeases
and numbs
more than
it awakens
and energizes
must be challenged.

126.

The job
of your soul
is not just to
inspire and
guide you,
but to challenge
and transform you.

127.

Wondrous things
happen when we
let the Spirit
dance away
on the floor
of our familiarities
and preferences.

128.

More Precious Moments

The treasure
in slowing down
is more
time and
space for
precious
moments.

129.

Unsung Calendar Dates

Spaces
to ponder
and wonder.
Places
to loiter
and saunter.

130.

God's Fingerprints

Anything that
opens
the mind or
softens
the heart has
God's fingerprints
all over it.

131.

Soul to Self:

Sometimes
you must
defiantly
walk away
from stress
and strain
and tenaciously
claim your calm.

132.

Essential Emptying

Moments of
emptying
are essential.

Rest
your
mind.

133.

You don't
just have
dreams;
you create
dreams.

What are you
dreaming
on purpose?

134.

I
Intentionally
access
my
soul power
to
create
daily.

135.

Ever
onward
with
intentional
purpose
and
glad
surprise.

136.

I am
clear,
confident
and
creative
and
expect to be.

137.

To
speak
life
is
to
spark
life.

138.

I
am
not
afraid
of
my
light.

139.

I look
my troubles
in the face
until they
soften and
teach me
something.

140.

I give
my
dreams
a
standing
ovation.

141.

Where there
are no
rests;
there is no
music.

142.

I pick
myself
up and
trust
my way
through.

143.

I dare
to
remain
true
to
my
vision
and
imagination.

144.

I will sign
a peace treaty
with
conditions
out of
my control.

145.

I vow
to keep
listening
to the
whispers
of my
soul.

146.

I
choose
to
tackle
the terror
of doing
something
new.

Also By Kirk Byron Jones

Rest in the Storm: Self-Care Strategies for Clergy and Other Caregivers
Addicted to Hurry: Spiritual Strategies for Slowing Down
The Jazz of Preaching: How to Preach with Great Freedom and Joy
Morning B.R.E.W.: A Divine Power Drink for Your Soul
The Morning B.R.E.W. Journal

Holy Play: The Joyful Adventure of Unleashing Your Divine Purpose
Say Yes to Grace: How to Burn Bright Without Burning Out
The Sacred Seven: How to Create, Manage, and Sustain a Fulfilling Life
Say Yes to Grace: The Facebook Page Reflections

Fulfilled: Living and Leading with Unusual Wisdom, Peace, and Joy
Refill: Meditations for Leading with Wisdom, Peace, and Joy
Grace Sparks: Short Reflections to Encourage, Enlighten, and Energize Your Spirit
Calling Forth New Life: Becoming Your Freshest, Finest, and Fullest Self
Calling Forth New Life: The In-Visioning Journal

Just Because You're in a Storm Doesn't Mean the Storm has to be in You
Yes to Grace: Short Inspirations to Refresh Your Soul
Soul Talk: How to Have the Most Important Conversation of All
Soul Talk Journal
Water to Wine: The Five Levels of Marvelous Change

Writing in the Open Window: Being Creative in Crisis
The Spiritual Treasure of Jazz: Wisdom that Will Make Your Life Swing!
Rest in the Storm: Self-Care Strategies for Clergy and Other Caregivers, 20th Anniversary Ed.
Rest in the Storm: The Creativity Journal
Soul to Self: Enchanting Wisdom from Within
Holy Play: The Joyful Adventure of Unleashing Your Divine Purpose